Tigers, Frogs, and Rice Cakes
A Book of Korean Proverbs

selected and translated by Daniel D. Holt

illustrated by Soma Han Stickler

SHEN'S
BOOKS

To my father and mother, who supported my love of Korea
even when it took me far away from them.
—D.D.H.—

To my mother, father, and husband, John.
—S.H.S.—

Special thanks to Song Que Hahn, who helped us understand
the many meanings of Korean proverbs.
—Publisher—

Text copyright ©1999 by Daniel D. Holt
Illustrations copyright ©1999 by Soma Han Stickler
All rights reserved.
This book, or parts thereof, may not be reproduced in any form or by any means
without written permission from the publisher.

Shen's Books
40951 Fremont Blvd
Fremont,CA 94538

(800)456-6660
http://www.shens.com

Printed in China
First Edition
10 9 8 7 6 5 4 3 2

Library of Congress Cataloging-in-Publication Data

Tigers, frogs, and rice cakes : a book of Korean proverbs /
selected and translated by Daniel D. Holt ; illustrated by Soma Han Stickler.
1st ed.
p. cm.
English and Korean
Summary: A concise collection of centuries old proverbs representing enduring values in Korean society,
followed by a brief explanation of the proverb and any English equivalent.
ISBN 1-885008-10-4
1. Proverbs, Korean. 2. Proverbs, Korean--Translations into English. [1. Proverbs, Korean. 2. Korean language
materials--Bilingual.] I. Holt, Daniel D., 1947- . II. Stickler, Soma Han, ill.
PN6519.K6T53   1998   398.9'957--dc21   98-7808   CIP   AC

Author's Note

The Korean word for proverb is *sok-dam* or "folk saying," implying a connection with the life of common people. Having survived for centuries, proverbs represent enduring values held throughout all strata of Korean society. Each proverb in this book focuses on a significant folk symbol or belief deeply regarded by Koreans. In a culture where language ability, particularly taciturnity, is highly respected, proverbs are used as a tool for expressing oneself with grace and style.

Korean proverbs represent a storehouse of useful information. By reminding us of basic truths, they help develop our capacity to live with compassion, perseverance, and responsibility. With humor and metaphor, they provide subtle, indirect ways to teach young people important lessons about personal integrity and cooperation. In addition, they provide a window on Korean culture and language. The simple elegance of proverbs helps us learn much about Korea by reading and understanding only a few words. By comparing proverbs across cultures, we can identify some of the similarities and differences that help us appreciate the diversity that characterizes the world.

Various systems have been developed for romanizing the Korean alphabet. Most of these methods are based on the internationally recognized system—McCune-Reischauer. This book uses an adaptation of the system to represent the way in which the words would actually be spoken. The romanization of the language is only an approximation of the way Koreans would pronounce the proverb in speech. To find the most accurate representation, ask a Korean to read the proverbs for you.

등잔 밑이 어둡다.

It is dark at the base of the lamp.

Teung-jan mi-chi eo-dup-tta.

칠전 팔기

Seven falls, eight rises.

Chil-jjeon pal-kki.

고추는 작아도 맵다!

Though it is small, the pepper is hot.

Ko-chu-neun cha-ga-do maep-tta.

가랑잎이 솔잎더러
바스락 거린다고 한다.

**The dry leaves tell the pine needle
it is rustling.**

*Ka-rang-ni-pi sol-lip-tteo-reo pa-seu-rak
keo-rin-da-go han-da.*

호랑이도 제 말하면 온다.

Speak of the tiger, and it appears.

Ho-rang-i-do che-mal-ha-myeon on-da.

개천에서 용 났다.

A dragon was born from a small stream.

Kae-cheon-e-seo yong na-tta.

우이 독경
Chanting into an ox's ear.

U-i tok kyeong.

개구리 올챙이적 생각 못한다.

The frog forgets its days as a tadpole.

*Kae-gu-ri ol-changi-jeok
saeng-gang mot-han-da.*

우물 안 개구리

A frog in a well.

U-mu-ran kae-gu-ri.

To catch the cub,
one must enter the tiger's cave.

호랑이 새끼를 잡으려면
호랑이 굴 속으로 들어가야 한다.

Ho-rang-i sae-kki-reul cha-beu-ryeo-myeon,
ho-rang-i kul-so-geu-ro teu-reo-ga-ya-han-da.

호랑이 없는 곳에 토끼가 왕이다.

Where there is no tiger,
the rabbit becomes king.

Ho-rang-i eom-neun-go-se
to-kki-ga wang-i-da.

When whales fight,
shrimps' backs are often broken.

고래 싸움에 새우 등 터진다.

*Ko-rae ssa-um-e
sae-u-deung teo-jin-da.*

오는 정이 있어야 가는 정이 있다.

**Love must be given
before it can be received.**

*O-neun cheong-i i-sseo-ya
ka-neun cheong-i it-tta.*

빈 수레가 더 요란하다.

An empty push cart makes more noise.

Pin su-re-ga teo yo-ran-ha-da.

Starting is half done.

시작이 반이다.

Shi-ja-ki pa-ni-da.

목수가 많으면 집을 무너 뜨린다.

Too many carpenters
knock over the house.

Mok-su-ga ma-neu-myeon
chi-beul mu-neo tteu-rin-da.

Licking the outside of a watermelon.

Su-bak keot hal-kki.

남의 떡이 더 크게 보인다.

Someone else's rice cake looks bigger.

Nam-eui tteo-gi teo keu-ge po-in-da.

금강산도 식후경

Even Diamond Mountain should be admired after eating.

Keum-gang-san-do shik-hu-gyeong.

둘이 먹다가 한 사람 죽어도 모른다.

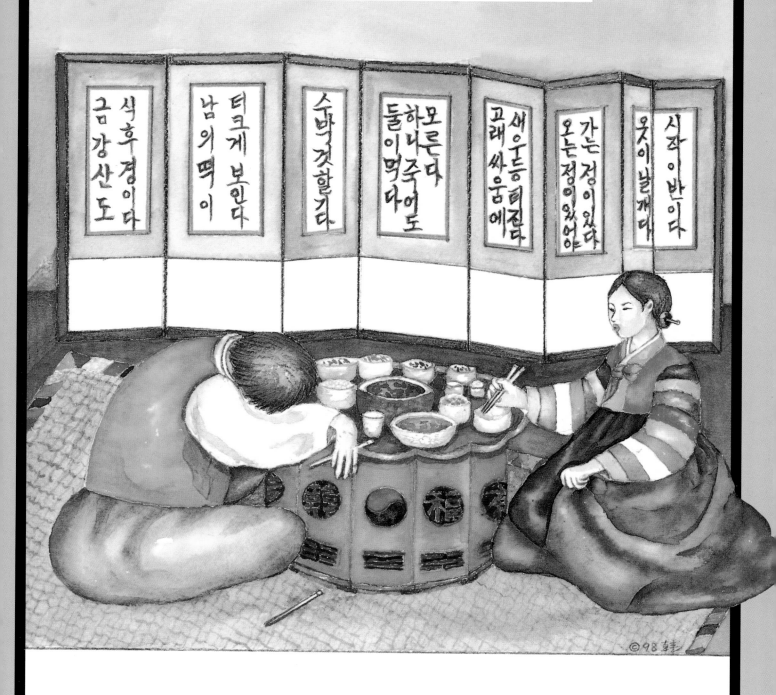

**While two are eating,
one wouldn't know even if the other dies.**

*Tu-ri meok-tta-ga han sa-ram
chu-geo-do mo-reun-da.*

Character

It is dark at the base of the lamp.

A lost item is most difficult to find when it is right in front of us. A related meaning is that we tend to know least about the affairs closest to us.

Seven falls, eight rises.

No matter how many times we fall, we must be determined to rise again. Setbacks help us develop the virtues of tenacity and perseverance. "If at first you don't succeed, try, try again."

Though it is small, the pepper is hot.

We should not judge people's ability to do great things based on their size, nor underestimate the inner strength of people with small stature. "Good things come in small packages."

The dry leaves tell the pine needle it is rustling.

Dry, autumn leaves rustle loudly in the wind but scold the tiny pine needle for being noisy. We are quick to find fault with others while unconscious of our own shortcomings. "See a speck in another's eye and not notice a log in one's own eye."

Speak of the tiger, and it appears.

Sometimes a person shows up just as we are talking about him/her. In such an apparently coincidental moment, we often feel the interconnectedness that holds us and everything else together.

A dragon was born from a small stream.

This proverb is used to describe a person from a poor background who became successful. Just as it is remarkable for a huge dragon to appear from a small stream, so it is to witness self-made people who overcome their humble beginnings and other forms of adversity.

Chanting into an ox's ear.

No matter how well-intended or reasoned our explanation, if the person does not have the background knowledge, interest, comparable experience, or readiness to listen, our effort may fall on deaf ears.

The frog forgets its days as a tadpole.

As we gain status, wealth, and power, we often forget people and experiences that helped us along the way.

A frog in a well.

A frog that lives its life in a well has a limited view of the world. This proverb is used to describe someone who is narrow-minded and inexperienced.

Cooperation and Accomplishment

To catch the cub, one must enter the tiger's cave.

To experience success, we must be willing to act in spite of our fears and to persevere in the face of difficulties. "Nothing ventured, nothing gained."

Where there is no tiger, the rabbit becomes king.

When the leader of a group is absent or weak, unqualified people sometimes try to take control, often making matters worse and more chaotic. Cooperation depends on people knowing themselves, assuming appropriate roles, and fulfilling their responsibilities with humility.

When whales fight, shrimps' backs are often broken.

The less powerful are always hurt when those with power are in conflict. The Vietnamese say, "When cows fight, flies get hurt."

Love must be given before it can be received.

Cheong in this proverb is translated as "love," not of the romantic type, but as the heartfelt bond one senses with another person. Koreans deeply cherish their concept of *cheong,* better understood as the "heart" in the empathetic expression, "My heart goes out to you." Koreans might say that you have *cheong* when you exhibit compassion—your response to recognizing another person's needs and feelings.

An empty push cart makes more noise.

Push carts are two-wheeled wagons that Koreans use for pushing or pulling small cargo. This proverb suggests that those who know the least are often the most talkative.

Starting is half done.

Once we begin a task, we are well on our way to completing it. Koreans often use this proverb to express optimism about finishing something successfully.

Too many carpenters knock over the house.

One needs to know when to get involved and when to step back. "Too many cooks spoil the broth."

Eating

Licking the outside of a watermelon.

This proverb is used to describe a person who believes or acts with certainty, but in fact has only superficial knowledge and understanding. Koreans value deeply education and experience, yet try to demonstrate what they know with humility and self-effacement. "Just scratching the surface."

Someone else's rice cake looks bigger.

When we envy what others have, we are directed away from looking deeply at ourselves and becoming aware of our own strengths. "The grass is always greener on the other side of the fence."

Even Diamond Mountain should be admired after eating.

Koreans attach great importance to good food and eating. They often greet each other by asking, "Have you eaten?" Thus, this proverb expresses the notion that eating should come first—even before sightseeing at Korea's Diamond Mountain, one of the most beautiful mountain ranges in the world. A related meaning is that we should deal with our basic needs before seeking luxuries.

While two are eating, one wouldn't know even if the other dies.

When eating a delicious meal, we are unaware of anything else. This proverb is often used to break the silence when people are focused on eating and not talking.